Bones and Groans

Jan Burchett and Sara Vogler were already friends when they discovered that they both wanted to write books for children – and that it was much more fun to write together. They meet every weekday for gossip, jokes and writing. If one is stuck for an idea, the other always comes up with something, or makes a cup of tea. They both have two children who are always their first audience.

Jan used to be a primary school teacher and lives in Essex. Sara used to be a midwife and lives in London.

All Little Terrors titles can be ordered at your local bookshop or
are available by post from Book Service by Post (tel: 01624 675137).

Little Terrors

Bones and Groans

Jan Burchett and Sara Vogler

Illustrated by Judy Brown

MACMILLAN
CHILDREN'S BOOKS

For Sarah, Jack, Mary and Tom Kelly
– and their golf club

First published 1998 by Macmillan Children's Books
a division of Macmillan Publishers Limited
25 Ecclestone Place, London SW1W 9NF
and Basingstoke

Associated companies throughout the world

ISBN 0 330 36815 X

1 3 5 7 9 8 6 4 2

A CIP catalogue record for this book is available from the British Library.

Typeset by SX Composing DTP, Rayleigh, Essex
Printed and bound in Great Britain by Mackays of Chatham plc, Kent

Chapter One

George Brussell pulled open the heavy front door of Little Frightley Manor and poked his freckled nose out into the thick fog. Everything looked very strange this morning. The huge grounds of his home were completely invisible. The driveway seemed to stop dead against a wall of greyness. He couldn't see the stone gateposts with their giant Brussels sprouts, the fanciful statues on the lawn, the marble poodle in the lake with the water spouting out of its top-knot, or even the portcullis just outside the front door. And the fog was getting thicker by the minute. It was as if no world existed beyond George's house. The ugly gargoyles on the battlements above his head, who usually looked as if they were going to be sick, were just shapeless blobs.

"Great!" thought George. He was about to step into the mist when a voice stopped him.

"Is that you letting the fog in, Georgie?" shouted his mother from the lounge. "The damp will get into the piano and ruin its electrics."

The electronic grand piano was Sharren Brussell's latest pride and joy. No one in the family could play, but the piano itself regularly entertained them with a selection from its seven thousand and twenty-three tunes. It could be anything from *All Things Bright And Beautiful* to *Zip-A-Dee-Doo-Dah*.

"I'm going out in the garden," yelled George. He slammed the door, rattling the brass Brussels sprout knocker, and plunged into the fog. He was off to see his friends – he had something to show them.

But as soon as George left the safety of the porch, he couldn't get his bearings. He could hear Mr Duster whistling as he worked somewhere in the grounds, but he had no idea where. If only he'd left the lights on in his bedroom, then at least he'd have known where the west wing was. He stumbled across the front courtyard and collided with something hard.

"Sorry!" he said, then he realized he was talking to the portcullis. It was a retired portcullis which just sat there in front of the house and wasn't any good at all against invaders. Today, however, it proved quite useful as George now knew where he was. He fumbled his way round it and aimed himself in the direction of the luxury caravan in the front garden where his friends lived. Most friends don't live in caravans in people's front gardens, but George's friends were different.

George felt his way round the outside of the caravan. He pulled his jacket over his head and, twisting his face into an expression rather like his favourite gargoyle, he burst in with a war cry. George could never get over how easy it was to scare his friends. But there was

3

Maggot gibbering under a table, his twin sister, Flo, trembling behind a curtain, and Mary escaping hurriedly through the skylight.

"It's only me," said George, grinning wickedly. "I've got something to show you."

Mary leapt down angrily and ran him through with her cutlass.

"Stop trying to kill me, Mary," laughed George, looking at the sword stuck in his belly. "It tickles."

Mary Ghoulstone was a nine-year-old pirate, with fierce eyebrows and a blood-stained shirt, who never missed her mark and had been feared throughout the Spanish Main from the time she was three. It was lucky for George that she was a ghost. She'd died long ago when Captain Redbeard, her mortal enemy, had stabbed her while she was looking the other way. She still had the ghost of his dagger in her chest.

Mary put her cutlass back in her belt and

pushed her wild brown spectral hair out of her eyes.

"How dare ye come aboard in that manner," she growled, "scaring the spectral stuffing out of . . . everyone else."

"Feathers in a flap!" squawked a one-eyed green parrot as he flew out of the oven and on to Mary's shoulder.

The parrot, named Duck by Mary when she was very young, had died at the hands of Redbeard's cabin boy, who forced him

to walk the plank blindfolded with his wings tied behind his back.

"You *are* a bunch of scaredy-ghosts!" chuckled George.

George was a most unusual ten-year-old. Unlike most people, he had no trouble at all seeing ghosts and wasn't frightened when he did. Not that these particular spectres were very scary – especially at the moment. Their normally bright shimmer was dull and wobbly, and even Mary was faint round the edges and more transparent than usual.

"I'm sorry I frightened you." George scrabbled in his jeans pocket. "I've discovered something really brill . . ."

"You didn't frighten *me*," said Maggot, crawling out from under the table and wiping his nose on the sleeve of his sooty sailor suit. He'd started a sniffle the day before he died and, if you die with a cold, you need hankies for eternity.

"Why did you hide then?" sneered Flo, with a flounce of her frizzled ringlets, hurriedly pretending she was dusting the curtains and not hiding behind them.

"I did not," said Maggot crossly.

"You did."

"Didn't!"

"Did!"

"Didn't. I was studying a spider."

"You weren't!" shouted Flo, her bright blue eyes flashing. "You're terrified of spiders."

The eight-year-old twins were always arguing – especially about which of them had blown up the old west wing of Little Frightley Manor, and themselves into the bargain, in 1857. They'd been fiddling with an invention of their eccentric father's, and both claimed they'd put the fatal bananas into the fuel. Maggot still had a whiff of burnt fruit about him.

"Who cares about spiders?" said George impatiently. "I want to show you . . ."

"Master Magnus! Miss Florence!" wheezed a shocked voice.

A nozzle appeared round the bathroom

7

door and Edgar Jay, the ghost of an elderly upright vacuum cleaner, trundled out. His ghostly eyes, the bolts at the top of his dust bag, frowned at them. The pattern that ran down the bag like a long haughty nose, was twitching in disapproval above his down-turned crease of a mouth.

"This is no way for members of the noble Ghoulstone family to behave," he huffed severely, wagging his nozzle at Maggot and Flo.

Edgar Jay was a loyal Ghoulstone retainer and had been horrified when the Brussells had moved in with a vengeance after the last Ghoulstone had died, turning the noble but rambling old ruin into a nasty, overdressed show-house with candelabras and Brussels sprouts everywhere. Although the little Ghoulstone spooks loved being with George, they refused to live in the same house as his parents. Sharren and Darren wouldn't see a ghost if it walked through them, but they were just too loud and gaudy for comfort.

So the seven little spooks lived in the caravan in the garden instead.

"Listen, you lot," said George impatiently, rummaging in his pocket. "I've got . . ."

"Morning, everyone!" squeaked a tiny voice from the corner.

"Hello, Slightly," said Maggot fondly. "Not hibernating today?"

The ghost of Slightly Flat-Hedgehog waddled across the carpet. He'd been sat on by a pot-bellied pig at the local zoo.

"Why isn't anyone listening to me?" demanded George, tugging at his spiky hair in despair. "Have you all got extra ectoplasm in your ears or something? I'm busting my blood vessels trying to tell you what I've found in my bedroom. Look at this! It was hanging on a hook just inside the chimney."

He produced a large, rusty key labelled in faded brown ink: *West Wing Tower, Top Floor*.

"But the question is," he went on,

"which west wing does it mean? The one
you blew up, or the one they built
afterwards."

He grinned wickedly at the ghosts. "Let's
go and find out!"

Chapter Two

A piece of ghostly paper appeared in front of George's face.

"Hello, Boss," said George to the air. "Coming with us?"

Thirteen-year-old Bartholomew Otherington-Smythe was too timid to be seen, even by his ghostly friends. They only knew he was there when one of his lists appeared. His latest one now shook in front of George's nose.

"Keep still, Boss," laughed George, attempting to focus on the quivering words. He knew better than to try and hold on to anything spectral – it would just pass through his fingers. It wasn't fair – the ghosts could pick up real things if they tried.

"I'll read it," said Flo, snatching the piece of ghostly paper.

The Key – as I see it
by Bartholomew Otherington-Smythe

1. *To place the key in the keyhole will necessitate entering our old home.*
2. *Eerie things have been known to happen in Little Frightley Manor.*
3. *In every room there are contraptions that buzz and ping when one is least expecting it.*
4. *The artificial moose head above the fireplace follows me with its eyes.*
5. *But worst of all – Mr and Mrs Brussell are there.*
6. *No offence, George.*

"We'll keep out of their way," promised George. "Dad'll be in his office, and Mum's glued to the telly watching *Elevenses*. She won't budge till half past twelve. Come on, let's go."

The ghosts looked at the caravan windows where the grey fog was swirling and trying to get in. They weren't sure which was more scary – staying by themselves wrapped in this eerie blanket, or going into the big old house to open an unknown door.

George always knew when they were scared. Their bright shimmer paled and sometimes they almost faded away. They were the ones who were supposed to do the haunting but George doubted that these weedy spectres could ever spook anyone out.

"Well, I'm off," he said. He was determined to discover what lay behind the locked door in the west wing tower, even though it wouldn't be as much fun on his own.

He opened the caravan door, letting the fog finger its way inside. This was too much for the little ghosts.

"Wait for the crew, George!" yelled Mary, cutlass at the ready.

"Sound the foghorn!" squawked Duck.

George led the little band of quivering spectres across the huge, ancient stone hall of Little Frightley Manor, towards the stairs. Mary skulked along behind George with Duck on her shoulder, Maggot was carrying Slightly, a pile of ghostly paper fluttered along in the air, and Flo held Edgar Jay tightly by the nozzle. The ghosts clutched each other nervously as the electric grandfather clock whirred and pinged the half-hour. The sounds of *Elevenses* wafted out from the lounge on their left, and the door of the utility room on the other side of the hall opened to reveal a mountainous pile of freshly ironed clothes on a pair of legs. A friendly round face appeared from behind the ironing.

"Hello, boyo," said Mrs Duster. "Having fun, are we?" She smiled genially round the hall.

George was never sure whether the motherly housekeeper could see his ghostly friends or not, but he had no intention of mentioning it to them – they'd never have come in the house again. He was probably just imagining it, although it was very

14

strange that she always held doors open until they'd all gone through.

"Lunch at twelve, is it?" She bustled off up the stone staircase.

"Is that you again, Georgie?" came Sharren's voice above the noise of the telly. "What have you been doing with yourself?"

George groaned. He'd hoped to avoid his mother – she was likely to shriek and frighten his friends straight out of a window.

He led them protesting into the palatial lounge where, across a great expanse of expensive carpet, Sharren lay on a huge sofa, painting her nails to match her red dressing gown, and watching a feature on "Homes of the Rich and Famous". Flo, who loved gadgets, plucked up courage and began to inspect the piano.

"I hope you've wiped your feet," said Sharren, without taking her eyes away from the screen.

Maggot checked the soles of his burnt

boots, and Duck cleaned his claws on the curtains. Edgar Jay began to blow gusts of air noisily out of his ghostly nozzle. This was all the hoovering he could manage since an accident with his wiring had left him on the scrap heap.

"There's still a draught in here," muttered Sharren, shivering as he passed. "Even though we've had those brand-new double-glazed Elizabethan windows put in."

Maggot clambered up on to Sharren's sofa. Sharren sniffed.

"Have you been at the bananas, George?" She turned back to the television. "Ooh, look at that. I've always wanted a maze."

Maggot walked along the back of the sofa, wobbling like a bad tightrope walker, came to the end and leapt at the nearest chair. He bounced higher than he meant to, sailed through the air and ended up dangling by his scorched trousers from the antlers of the moose head over the fireplace. Flo snorted with laughter as Mary climbed up on the mantelpiece to rescue him.

"Come down," sighed George.

Sharren stared at him. "Why are you talking to the moose, Georgie?" she asked. "Go and watch a video if you're bored."

Flo, her mucky face alight with mischief, pressed a piano key experimentally. *Silent Night* blasted out. Flo fell backwards off the piano stool in a flurry of singed

petticoats. Mary dropped Maggot into the fireplace and drew her cutlass. Edgar Jay gave a gasp of surprise and almost sucked up one of Boss's lists, while Slightly rolled into a scroll.

"Enemy attack!" squawked Duck, flapping up to the chandelier in alarm.

"Did you leave the piano timer on?" asked Sharren suspiciously.

George shook his head dumbly. He didn't dare speak in case he started giggling. Sharren patted her lacquered blond hair back into place and turned back to the screen where a champagne Jacuzzi was being shown. She let out a shriek of admiration that rattled the ornaments.

That was enough for the little ghosts. With a rush of air that made the curtains flap, they bounded silently across the carpet towards the closed door which led to the west wing. It was at times like this that the ghosts wished they could float like grown-up ghouls, but all they could manage was a peculiar bouncing run that made them look like astronauts on the moon. With a spectral pop they whooshed through the wooden door.

George was impressed. The little spectres hardly ever got through solid objects on the first try.

"Thought you little terrors weren't so keen to go exploring!" he laughed as he joined them in the corridor leading to his dad's study and the spiral staircase of the tower.

"Better the unknown horrors of the west wing," huffed Edgar Jay, "than to endure a battering on the eardrums by Mrs Brussell!"

George's dad worked from home. The door of his study was open, and George could see the plump shape of his father, busy at his computer.

"Hello, Dad!" said George brightly, poking his head round the door.

Darren hurriedly flicked off *Killer*

Kangaroos where he'd got to level forty-one for the first time ever.

"Er . . . just e-mailing Australia, son," he spluttered. "Very busy. Got to get on."

George loved catching his dad out and listening to what excuse he would come up with each time. He sometimes wondered how his father managed to make so much money when he seemed to spend most of his time playing computer games. He led the ghosts towards the stairs. Darren, meanwhile, was staring at a list that had appeared on a piece of his paper in the fax tray.

The situation in Australia – as I see it
by Bartholomew Otherington-Smythe

1. *The kangaroos seem to be exceedingly dangerous.*
2. *I would not advise anyone to stay in the room with them.*
3. *Or indeed in the same country.*
4. *Act immediately.*
5. *Or even sooner.*

Darren scratched his bald patch. He thought he'd better e-mail his office in Australia after all.

George switched on the lights and led the way up the circular stone staircase, followed by Flo who dragged Edgar Jay by the nozzle. Maggot and Mary shoved him from behind.

"I say," wheezed the elderly hoover as his wheels rattled, "steady on."

Any self-respecting ghost would have

floated its way up by now, thought George impatiently. But then nothing was straightforward where his spectral pals were concerned.

At last they arrived at the small landing that led to George's bedroom. The ghosts looked wistfully at George's door with its sign:

Please do not pass through this door without knocking!

It was the only part of the house they enjoyed being in. George had everything any child could wish for in his bedroom. Flo never tired of the computer, Slightly loved hibernating in George's football bag, and Mary and Duck had made a crow's-nest in the canopy of his four-poster bed.

"Only one more floor," said George cheerfully, setting off into the dark. There were no lights leading to the top of the tower, and the little ghosts paled as they listened to his footsteps on the stone stairs.

"Couldn't we stay down here?" whispered Maggot, wiping his runny nose anxiously on his sleeve and hiding behind Mary.

"Scaredy-spook!" taunted Flo.

"Am not!"

"Yes you are!"

"Not!"

"You are!"

"Quit your quarrelling," growled Mary, "or I'll have your guts for garters! I'm going." And she strode up the stairs, pushing Maggot up in front of her.

George reached the top where, in the shadows, there stood a heavy, carved door with an old and rusty keyhole. He waited for the quivering band to join him. Then, with a flourish, he produced the key and put it in the lock.

"Wow!" he exclaimed. "It fits!" He struggled to turn it. "I don't think this door has been opened for years!"

"I believe it was locked even before I arrived at Little Frightley Manor,"

23

wheezed Edgar Jay. "Of course, I was the downstairs hoover and never ventured up here." He scratched the top of his bag with his nozzle. "But now I come to think of it, there was some talk about this room. Yes, I remember! There were tales of unearthly groans and rattling skeletons."

"Why didn't you say so before?" said Flo anxiously. "We'd have stayed in the caravan."

"Great!" exclaimed George, happily. "Maybe the house *is* haunted after all. Someone probably leapt to their death from a window, or better still, got walled up in there!"

"Let's go down to your bedroom," quavered Maggot, sniffing hard and pulling himself away from Mary's iron grip.

"Below deck!" squawked Duck hopefully from the shadows.

"Even your parents haven't tried to get in," said Flo nervously. "So there must be something really awful in there!" She began to back down the stairs.

"My mum and dad wouldn't notice if Phantom of the Year was standing in front of them and pulling faces," laughed George. "They haven't been up here because they can't agree what to do with the room. In fact, it's caused some right royal squabbles. Mum want a solarium, and Dad wants an observatory, though I can't think why – to him the Plough and the Bull are just local pubs!"

George spat on his hands and grasped the key firmly, twisting it with all his strength. At first nothing happened, but at last there was a grating sound, followed by a loud clunk. George took hold of the rusty old door handle and turned it. With a long, shuddering creak, the door opened.

Chapter Three

George stepped boldly into the room at the top of the tower and peered around in the gloom. The new wing with its tower had been built by Maggot and Flo's older brother, after they'd blown up the old west wing. Sir Cedric Ghoulstone had grand ideas and rather fancied the castle look, but by the time Bodgers the Victorian Builders started work on the top of the tower, he'd run out of money. So the room had only two narrow windows, which were little more than slits, bare boards on the floor, no ceiling – and Cedric's dream turret was just a pathetic little pointed roof. The room was dusty and full of cobwebs, and any light which the windows let in was dulled by the fog. Apart from a few battered old crates lying about on the floorboards, it appeared to be empty.

"There's nothing to be afraid of here," said George, disappointed. "Come and see."

His pale, phantom friends slowly made their way in and looked around nervously, while Boss's pile of ghostly paper trembled in the doorway. Edgar Jay blew the dust off one of the crates. Mary checked everywhere for enemies, and Duck bravely flew over to one of the windows and peered out of the slit with his good eye. He'd lost his other eye in a small dispute with a swordfish. Slightly struggled out of Maggot's arms and started snuffling round a crate. Flo sneaked a look inside it.

"Spooktacular!" she exclaimed, pulling out a peacock-feathered fan, a golden goblet and three ugly stuffed monkeys. "It's a treasure-trove!"

George came to join her.

"Wow!" he shouted, his face lighting up. "What a find! There's things from all over the world here."

"That rings a bell," wheezed Edgar Jay.

"This could be the fabled and famous collection of Sir Albert Ghoulstone."

Edgar Jay could relate the whole seven hundred year history of the illustrious family, from Sir Philip the Crusader, who built the house and died in a desperate duel with a relative, to Lady Cecily, who perished when a portrait fell on her head. He turned to the twins. "He was, of course, the son of your brother, Sir Cedric, and therefore your nephew."

"Uncle Maggot!" giggled Flo.

Maggot glared at her.

"As I was saying," huffed the old hoover, irritated at the interruption, "your nephew, Sir Albert, was a renowned explorer. It was rumoured that he acquired many strange and wondrous possessions from his expeditions around the world."

Sir Albert Ghoulstone had indeed acquired many strange and wondrous possessions, but not so much from his expeditions around the world as from his nocturnal expeditions into other people's houses, castles and the odd museum. He was always popping off "exploring" and coming back laden with goodies. One evening in 1923 he kissed his daughter, Cecily, and told her he was going to the Himalayas for a spot of mountain-climbing. He locked all his latest loot in the tower room, away from prying eyes, and hid the key that George found up his bedroom chimney. That night Sir Albert fell to his death – not from the top of a lofty peak into a ravine, but from the roof of the Tower of London, head first into a bucket. He'd been after the crown jewels. His ghost, with its bucket on its head and empty swag bag under its arm, joined the many distinguished and supposedly headless spooks which haunt the famous landmark.

The tower room remained locked, and stories about it grew over the years. Servants would claim they heard moans that could only come from beyond the grave, and so no one dared break the lock and enter. Of course, when Lady Cecily, his daughter and last of the line, died, and her faithful retainer retired to the seaside, there was no one to tell the Brussells about the history of the strange room at the top of the tower. Not that Sharren and Darren would have been interested. Anything odd about Little Frightley Manor they either blamed on George or on the renovations of Bodgers the Builders.

"I wonder where he got this?" gasped George, pulling out a fearsome mask and putting it in front of his face. "I bet it's a death mask or something to frighten off spirits."

He advanced on the ghosts to test it out. Flo giggled at the big staring eyes, the blue hair that sprouted everywhere, and the painted mouth wide open to show sharp yellow teeth. George looked like a demon in jeans.

"I bet it came from some oriental temple or palace," said George from behind the mask.

Actually, Sir Albert had acquired it during a night-time raid on Woolworth's.

Maggot stuck his head in the crate and came out sneezing, with a dagger covered in dusty jewels.

"I challenge you, you ugly . . . atishoo . . . monster," he shouted, waving the dagger at the demon. Mary leapt into the fray with some dazzling swordplay, and Flo defended herself with a painted plate. Some ghostly paper missiles, aimed from the doorway, flew past the mask.

"Mind your ankles!" squawked Duck, as Slightly emerged from the crate, brandishing a diamond-studded hatpin in his front claws.

"*En garde!*" squeaked Slightly.

Suddenly, above the din, they heard a strange groan. The ghosts stopped mid-fight and Flo dropped her china shield, which smashed on the floor.

"Pieces of plate!" squawked Duck, in alarm.

George took the mask off, and the

little ghosts shimmered and virtually disappeared. A nervous list materialized.

The Dusty Room – As I see it
by Bartholomew Otherington-Smythe

1. *The stories about the bones and the groans must be true.*
2. *There could be something unspeakable here.*
3. *I will make my usual suggestion as to the action we should take.*
4. *Run away.*
5. *Immediately.*
6. *Be careful on the stairs.*

"It's coming from behind the door!" said George, excitedly.

"Let's go!" shouted Maggot, but before the ghosts could move, George had flung the door shut to reveal a long object leaning against the wall and covered in a dusty oilcloth. He pulled the cloth away.

"Zowie!" he gasped as he gazed at the treasure he'd discovered.

There, standing before him, covered in

32

beautiful hieroglyphics, and marching lines of skinny men in loincloths with tea towels on their heads, was a magnificent box in the shape of a human body.

"It's an Egyptian coffin!" he exclaimed, gazing at the elaborately painted face. "It could have a mummy inside."

"Why would your mother be inside there?" asked Flo.

"Not *my* mum!" explained George. "*A* mummy."

"Whose mummy?" asked Maggot.

"I had no idea mothers lived in cupboards," said Edgar Jay. "I thought it was only vacuum cleaners. But of course, not having had a mother, I am no expert on their behaviour. Although I must say it is a very fine cupboard."

"A mummy," said George patiently, "is a body all wrapped in bandages. In ancient Egypt if you were dead important – or rather, dead *and* important – that's what they did with your corpse. Then the mummy got put in a coffin like this one and plonked in a pyramid. People go on trips to see them now."

"I knew that!" said Flo.

"No you didn't!" sneered Maggot.

"I did!"

"Didn't!"

"Did!"

"Shut up!" interrupted George. "I'm going to see what's inside."

"Let me run me cutlass through it first," growled Mary, pulling it out from her belt.

"Don't be daft!" laughed George. "B
you couldn't even get your hand through
the wood."

"I could!" shouted Mary, always one to
take up a challenge. She pressed her fingers
against the surface of the coffin and then
pushed her hand through the thick wooden
lid. With a tremendous effort, she forced
her arm in up to her elbow and smiled
triumphantly. Then, all at once, she yelped
and pulled her arm back very quickly.

"There be something in there," she
said urgently. "I could feel it. It were
horrible . . ."

Suddenly they heard a dreadful
thumping. The little spectres almost
vanished through the floor in fright as
something large and loud burst into the
room.

Chapter Four

Something large, loud and waving a fax. It was Darren.

"George!" he shouted, taking no notice of the mess on the floor. "Do you know anything about kangaroos running amok in Melbourne? Have you been messing about . . .?"

He caught sight of the coffin and stopped, opening and closing his mouth like a rather dim goldfish. Before George had a chance to speak, a ghostly and rather agitated list was thrust in front of his eyes. He read it surreptitiously.

Manners as I see them
by Bartholomew Otherington-Smythe

1. *Your father has just walked straight through me.*
2. *He did not say excuse me or sorry.*

3. *I consider that very ill-mannered of him.*
4. *I know he is completely unaware of my presence, but even so I am somewhat miffed.*

"Sorry, Boss," said George to the doorway.

"Don't be sorry, son," breathed Darren, forgetting all about the Australians and whipping out his mobile phone from the pocket of his purple tracksuit trousers. "Just wait till your mother sees this!"

He quickly punched in some numbers.

"Sharren . . . is that you, darling? . . . What? . . . The reception's dreadful up here . . . No, of course I'm not on the roof . . . You'll never believe what I've found" – he caught George's eye – "what our lad's found at the top of the tower. You've got to come and see it, Shazza . . . It's not that much of a climb . . . You can watch *Elevenses* at any time!"

He clicked Sharren off, mid-complaint. After a few minutes, they heard distant mutterings and the tip-tap of high heels as she climbed the stairs.

"This had better be worth it, Darren," she was complaining. "I'm worn out! We need a lift up here. Do you realize I'm missing . . ." She suddenly saw the coffin. The ghosts put their fingers in their ears.

"Ooooooh!!" she shrieked.

"Isn't it wonderful, darling?" said Darren, stroking the wood. "Looks genuine, and I know the perfect place to show it off – the lounge."

"I'm not having it down there!" shrilled Sharren. "It won't go with the moose head or the juke box."

"But, Sharren, we could redecorate. I can see it now – pyramids and stuffed camels . . ."

"Never mind what you can see, Darren Brussell," said Sharren crossly as her husband tapped the coffin lid. "I'm off to see the end of *Elevenses*." She tottered out, with a sweep of her red dressing gown.

"But, *sweet*heart," called Darren,

lumbering straight through Maggot as he went after her, "all the neighbours would flock round . . . We'd be the talk of the village . . . We could be in *Hi There!* Magazine."

The sounds of the argument died away.

"Your parents are so squabblesome, George," said Flo smugly.

"And large," groaned Maggot, re-arranging his spectral stuffing.

But George wasn't listening. He was staring mournfully at the painted face on the carved wood.

"What a shame," he said. "I thought there might be a body inside."

"But your father said it was a genuine coffin," huffed Edgar Jay.

"If Dad thinks it's genuine," sighed George, "it's got to be a fake."

"But there be something in there," said Mary, rubbing her hand.

"You must have imagined it," said George. "Let's go. Mrs Duster will be calling me for lunch."

"I would suggest a spot of tidying first," wheezed Edgar Jay, whose bag got in a flap whenever he saw a mess. He tried to blow the broken pieces of china into a heap.

George wasn't the sort of boy who enjoyed tidying, but he thought they'd be able to have some fun with the treasures later, and he didn't want his parents taking them off to decorate the house. He put the mask carefully into its crate and tried to persuade Slightly to give up his hatpin, then he pushed the boxes into the shadows.

Flo was just clearing up the last piece of plate when they all heard a faint tapping noise. It was coming from the coffin!

"Is that Edgar Jay in there?" asked Maggot. "He said it was a nice cupboard."

"Perhaps he's trying it out," suggested Flo.

"I'm over here actually," wheezed the old hoover from behind the crates, "tidying up – as you should be."

"Then who made the noise in the coffin?" quavered Maggot.

"It's probably death-watch beetle," said George, putting his ear to the wood.

"Sounds like lunch," squeaked Slightly, licking his lips.

"It be bigger than a beetle, mark my words," warned Mary, stepping back and bumping into Maggot, who was making for the door. "I reckon it be a monster and we'll all be *his* lunch."

Slightly squealed and scuttled off to a dark corner. He decided it would be safer to hibernate for a bit.

George took hold of the coffin lid.

"Don't open it!" yelled Maggot from the doorway.

"It'll only be a load of old dead bones," said George, puffing with the effort as he pulled.

The coffin stayed firmly shut. George put his foot on the wall and heaved. The lid opened a crack and an eerie yellow light shone through the gap.

"Close it while you have the chance!" yelled Flo, crouching down behind a crate.

But George wasn't going to give up just because his friends were going wobbly around the edges. He gave one last tug and fell backwards as the door of the coffin swung open. George and the ghosts watched mesmerized as, wrapped from head to toe in bandages and with arms stretched menacingly towards them, a pale, transparent figure stepped out.

It was the ghost of an Egyptian mummy.

Chapter Five

The mummy stood there for a moment, glowing with a yellow light. It was no taller than George, and was covered in roughly torn strips of linen, with a narrow slit for a mouth and two deep eye holes.

The bandaged figure lurched towards the terrified ghosts who almost vanished with fright. Then, suddenly, the mummy swung round stiffly and staggered through the doorway. It put its left leg straight out, stepped forwards, and fell head first down the winding stairs like a skittle.

George raced after it, and without thinking Flo and Maggot followed, catching up as the mummy crashed into George's bedroom door and slid to the floor. Mary followed, dragging Edgar Jay behind her, Duck swooped down above their heads and a pile of ghostly papers flapped timidly at the rear. With great difficulty, Flo and Maggot heaved the stiff, swathed figure to its feet and brushed it down, trying not to laugh. They'd forgotten all about being scared – this ghost was obviously no better at floating than them.

George opened his bedroom door, and Flo and Maggot lifted the mummy into the room and propped it against George's four-poster bed.

"Are you all right, Sir . . . or . . . Madam?" wheezed Edgar Jay as he blew the dust off the figure.

The mummy sneezed through its bandages, groaned and tried to rub its head with a stiff arm.

"I do not recognize this chamber," said a faint voice through the slit in the wrappings. "What has happened?"

"Wow!" said George, trying to see inside the eye holes. "You're no fake!"

The figure's eyes widened inside the holes.

44

"Indeed not!" he snapped. His voice was posh and had a slight foreign accent. "I am a king. I was Pharaoh of all Egypt. Can't you tell by my golden aura?"

Flo immediately curtseyed, Maggot bowed, and Duck stood to attention and saluted. Mary, eyeing the figure suspiciously, fingered her cutlass. Kings, in her experience, had treasure ships and didn't look too kindly upon pirates.

"Oh, your majesty," huffed Edgar Jay, who would have knelt if he had knees. "You are most welcome."

Edgar Jay was overwhelmed. Throughout its long and illustrious history, Little Frightley Manor had never entertained a monarch before. Henry VIII had intended to visit Sir Walter Ghoulstone in 1536, but cancelled at the last minute as one of his wives needed beheading.

The mummy tried to pose regally in front of them. But it's difficult to be regal when you're wrapped in bandages and stiff as a board, and George snorted with laughter.

"How dare you mock a monarch?" shouted the ghost pharaoh. "By the beak of the god Thoth, I will have your insides cut out and thrown to the jackals!"

"Tripe and onions!" squawked Duck.

"Just you try it," muttered Mary, drawing her cutlass.

"Look," explained George quickly before a fight broke out, "you're not in your royal court now, you know. We don't do disembowelling these days, and anyway, there aren't any jackals in Little Frightley Village."

The mummy gave a deep sigh and seemed to sag. Although his face was bandaged, he managed to look very sorry for himself.

"I apologize," he said mournfully. "The trouble is, I don't know how to behave regally." Then he giggled. "I was only king for three weeks before Uncle Phatchops pushed me off a pyramid."

"Wow!" said George, impressed. "Did you bash your brains in? . . . Hang on a minute," he added, frowning. "If you died falling off a pyramid, why doesn't your ghost look all battered? I mean, look at Mary, she's still got the fatal dagger in her chest, and Flo and Maggot are all charred. Surely the ancient Egyptians only got wrapped up *after* they were dead." A delighted gleam came into George's eyes. "Perhaps they embalmed you while you were still alive!"

"You could be right," said the figure. "Uncle Phatchops was in a hurry to get me off a pyramid and into one."

"I bet I am right," said George. "That's why you're a mummy."

"Mummy?" asked the small pharaoh. "I am a twelve-year-old boy, not a mother!"

"A mummy," explained George, "is an Egyptian body all . . . Oh, never mind . . . I'm George Brussell. You'll have heard my parents, Sharren and Darren Brussell. They were the ones who were arguing about your coffin. You're best off avoiding them. And this motley lot are the ghosts of Little Frightley Manor."

"I am King Tootingkommon," said the mummy grandly. "I live with my sister Ramesestreet, my father Klappum-kommon, my mother Kommonasmuk, and Cleo . . ." He suddenly stopped and grinned. "I don't often get ghosts coming to visit. And come to think of it," he added, pointing a stiff arm at George, "you're the first living person who has seen me. Most visitors just gawp at our empty coffins and wonder what the hieroglyphics mean . . ."

"Have I missed something?" asked a little voice from the door. Slightly had woken up from his five-minute hibernation and, finding himself alone in the tower room, had scuttled down in search of his friends, still clutching his hatpin. He suddenly spotted the strange, bandaged apparition and sniffed at its feet.

"Must have been run over!" he squeaked smugly.

Slightly was proud that he had avoided the fate of most hedgehogs, and felt very superior to those who hadn't. He

48

clambered up on to George's bed, rolled himself into a tube, and went back to sleep.

"I'd be grateful," continued Tooting-kommon, taking no notice of the interruption, "if you would reunite me with my family. They can't be far away. It is the chamber with the three other open coffins, some wooden gods scattered about, and my mother's jewellery all over the place. Perhaps you can tell me why my coffin lid was closed and the coffin was moved. It was ever so bumpy."

"Why didn't you escape and stay with your family?" asked Flo.

Tootingkommon's mouth-slit drooped in embarrassment. "I'm not very good at going through wood."

The ghosts nodded sympathetically. The coffin lid was very thick and to get all your spectral stuffing through would be extremely difficult and would feel most unpleasant.

A quivering list appeared from George's underpants drawer. Flo read it out loud.

Misunderstandings as I see them
by Bartholomew Otherington-Smythe

1. His majesty appears to be under the misapprehension that this is his home.
2. Someone had better inform him that he is miles from his abode.
3. Probably thousands of miles.
4. I believe he must have been discovered by Sir Albert Ghoulstone in a pyramid in Egypt and brought to Little Frightley Manor.
5. Perhaps someone had better tell his majesty

that his family are not here.

6. *Somehow we must package him up and send him back to them.*

7. *I suggest the Royal Mail.*

"You mean I'm not at home?" whimpered the little pharaoh. "I thought this was just another chamber."

But the ghosts and George weren't listening. They were still poring over Boss's list.

"How are we going to wrap him?" said Maggot. "He's a ghost like us."

"He be wrapped already," said Mary in a surly voice. "All we need is a stamp. Let's do it now."

"But Mary!" shouted Maggot. "We don't know the address of his pyramid!"

"We could use George's encyclopaedia," said Flo eagerly. "The one on his computer."

"Not at home?" Tootingkommon was repeating in a daze.

"An encyclopaedia won't help!" Maggot

snapped at his sister. "It hasn't got addresses in it."

"We've got to find *some* way to help him," shouted Flo. "Don't be such a wet blanket, Maggot!"

"I'm not!"

"Yes you are!"

"Not!"

"You are!"

"I am not!"

Suddenly there was an unearthly howl. Everyone fell silent and looked at the little pharaoh.

"I want to go home!" wailed Tooting-kommon. "*I want my mummy!*"

Chapter six

George sat in the kitchen, hunched over his beans on toast, racking his brains to think of a way to return Tootingkommon to his family in Egypt. He'd left the ghosts in his bedroom, trying to find out exactly where the pharaoh's home was. Flo was searching through the section on Ancient Egypt in the computer encyclopaedia, Boss was making a list of overseas postal rates, and Mary was sitting on George's bed, next to the snoring hedgehog, leafing through George's history book, *The Ghastly Past*. She was secretly trying to find out where a pharaoh kept his treasure. However, she wasn't getting very far. As she couldn't read, she had the book upside down and open on the chapter on Florence Nightingale and her bandages.

Maggot and Duck were watching *The*

Mummy's Revenge on George's television. Maggot said it would give them some clues and the king might recognize something, but Tootingkommon was quaking unhelpfully behind a chair with Edgar Jay obligingly covering His Majesty's eye holes with his nozzle during the scary bits.

George had wanted to stay and help them but he was too hungry. It was all right for the ghosts – they didn't need to eat, although they were usually willing to try one of Mrs Duster's cakes. Fortunately, anything a ghost eats disappears once it's inside its mouth, otherwise bits of half-chewed food would have been seen floating all over the place.

"Have a doughnut, boyo," said Mrs Duster, coming over to George with a plate. "I baked them specially."

Mrs Duster's doughnuts were Maggot's favourite.

"Take an extra one for . . . later," she smiled.

"Thanks, Mrs D."

George grabbed a couple and dashed off, through the utility room and up the narrow wooden staircase to the first-floor gallery. He leaned over the ornately carved banister and looked down into the hall to check his mother wasn't around. She'd only moan about jam on her carpets and take his doughnuts away.

He sped round the gallery, along a corridor and into the Victorian tower. He opened his bedroom door and sighed. The gruesome mummy on the television screen was throttling someone wearing baggy shorts and a silly hat. And, cowering behind the curtains of the four-poster bed, watching through their fingers, were his friends. The little spooks shuddered as the film came to its usual grisly end.

"You look as if you've done loads of research," said George sarcastically.

"We did find a reference to Tooting-kommon's tomb." Flo bounced off the bed defiantly.

"It's in the Valley of the Kings," added Maggot. "But we don't know which pyramid."

"That pesky thing," growled Mary, pointing at the computer. "It doesn't give any map bearings."

"It was all lies anyway," added Flo. "It said that King Tootingkommon fell ill and died, and that his uncle Phatchops mourned him for ever. It should have said Tootingkommon fell and died, and that his uncle Phatchops murdered him!"

George turned his *Ghastly Past* book the right way up and looked at the correct page for the Ancient Egyptians. It showed a mummified body – completely wrapped in white linen with no arms or legs showing.

"Hey!" he said, holding up the book and looking around for the ghostly pharaoh. "It's lucky they didn't bandage you like this. You wouldn't have been able to move at all."

"His uncle probably got it done on the cheap," said Maggot, scornfully.

Indeed, Tootingkommon had not been embalmed by an expert. Uncle Phatchops had been in a bit of a hurry to get the boy buried and said that only he should embalm his beloved nephew. If anyone else had seen the body, they would have known that King Tootingkommon had not died of spotty desert fever as Phatchops claimed. Phatchops was not a trained embalmer, but he'd been in the Desert Scouts and knew a little about first aid, so he had torn up his bedcovers and got to work.

George looked round the room. "Where is he?" he asked. "Where's King Toot?"

The ghosts searched under the computer, in the cupboards and on top of the four-poster bed. There was no sign of the ghostly mummy anywhere.

"We have to find him," said George urgently. "He can't have gone far. It'll be quicker if we split up!"

The little spooks looked horrified.

"Excuse me, Master George," wheezed Edgar Jay in alarm, "but that won't do our spectral stuffing any good at all."

"No, you daft lot," sighed George. "I don't mean . . . Never mind, let's search the house in pairs and then meet up in the hall."

"That's a much better idea, young sir," puffed Edgar Jay, happily. But the other ghosts were going wobbly round the edges, and Boss's papers were flapping nervously at the thought of going around the house without George.

Edgar Jay looked at them severely.

"My dear young Ghoulstones," he huffed solemnly. "Surely you are not too scared to help a fellow phantom in trouble? Take my nozzle, please, Miss Florence, and help me down to the ground floor. We'll start with the lounge."

The ghosts looked sheepish.

"Duck and me will steer a course to the cabins," muttered Mary, pulling out her spyglass.

"Maggot and Slightly will give you a hand," said George. "Oh, Maggot, I forgot." He thrust a sticky doughnut into Maggot's hand.

Maggot grinned, took a huge bite, scooped up the snoring Slightly and followed Mary off to the bedrooms.

"Toot won't have managed to climb the stairs in those bandages," said George to himself, "so I'd better help look downstairs."

A list appeared.

My Part in the search for the Pharaoh
by Bartholomew Otherington-Smythe

1. What is it?
2. My part, I mean.
3. Bearing in mind that I am too scared to enter any of the rooms on my own.
4. Perhaps I could co-ordinate the hunt from the hall.
5. From inside the downstairs toilet, I mean.

"Good idea, Boss," said George. "See you there . . . I mean, I won't *see* you there . . . Well, you know what I mean!"

Ten minutes later, everyone had joined Boss in the toilet. It was a bit of a squash for the ghosts. George read out the list that Boss had just completed on a piece of pink toilet paper.

Results of the Search
by Bartholomew Otherington-Smythe

1. The bedrooms are empty of ghostly pharaohs.
2. The lounge is phantom-free.

3. The kitchen and utility room are completely lacking in spooks.
4. The dining room has no glimpse of a ghoul.
5. Mr Brussell's study and conference room bear no evidence of Egyptians, ancient or otherwise.
6. In complete contrast, this toilet is bursting at the seams with spectres.
7. And Edgar Jay has his nozzle up my nose.

"I apologize, Master Bartholomew," huffed Edgar Jay, whacking Maggot around the head as he moved his nozzle. "Master Magnus, I am so sorry!" He tried to stick his nozzle in the corner and winded Flo on the way. "Forgive me, Miss Florence!" he wheezed apologetically.

George opened the door, and the ghosts tumbled out in a spectral heap. "We'll have to look outside," he decided.

"In the fog?" wailed Flo and Maggot together, picking themselves up.

"We'll stick together," said George, "and I don't mean with glue, Edgar Jay!"

The fog was as thick as ever as George

led the line of ghosts out of the front door and across the courtyard.

"We'll never spy anything in this pesky sea mist," growled Mary.

Maggot's nose was running more than usual. "This fog is a right pea-souper," he coughed.

"Sea-souper!" squawked Duck.

They crept past the portcullis and on to the lawn. George purposely steered them away from the caravan so that they didn't make a bolt for it.

"What's that?" squeaked Slightly, who was very alarmed to wake up and find himself being carried through the fog. He pointed a quivering paw at some white shapes that were looming ahead.

"They're just Mum's statues!" laughed George. "Well, three are hers and one's Dad's."

"But I can see five!" quavered Flo, fading into the fog with fright.

There in front of them was a marble-effect shepherdess with a lamb, a wood nymph with some flowers, an angel with a harp, and an autographed statue of Darren's favourite England striker with a football. And faintly shivering in the middle was a small bandaged figure with a golden aura.

The ghosts rushed over to the phantom pharaoh.

"I got lost looking for my family," whimpered the mummy. "And now I have strayed too far from my coffin. I'm fading away."

"It's the usual spectral gravity problem, is it?" sighed George. "You young ghosts! Come on, let's get you indoors. Now, we've got to work out how to get your *coffin* back to Egypt as well."

At that moment, there was the sound of crunching footsteps on the gravel drive.

"Before you start going wobbly," George told them firmly, "that'll be my dad. Can't you hear him puffing? He's had to walk to the pub – and back."

"But your dad *never* walks," said Flo in amazement.

"I know it sounds unbelievable," laughed George, "but he'd rather walk than risk driving the Rolls in this fog."

"Hello there, son," boomed Darren, looming out of the mist. "What are you doing out in this weather talking to yourself?" He rubbed his hands together. "I know it sounds unbelievable, but I had to walk to the Plough rather than risk driving the Rolls in this fog."

They set off back to the house. The little

64

ghosts carried the weedy bandaged figure, Maggot at his head, Flo at his feet, and Duck sitting on his chest.

"Homeward bound!" the parrot squawked cheerfully.

"Dad," said George, "you know that coffin in the tower? We should send it back to Egypt where it belongs."

"You don't need to worry about the coffin," said Darren, smiling smugly. "It's sorted. I got talking to two decent blokes in the pub and you won't believe it! It turned out they're experts on Egyptol . . . Egyptolly . . . on pyramids and things. They work for a magazine called *Mummies Monthly*, and they're coming here this very afternoon to do an article on us. Your mother will be ecstatic!"

"We can send it back afterwards," said George anxiously. "Can't we?"

"We won't have to bother, son," said Darren, opening the front door. "They told me these things are worth a lot of money so I've decided to sell it!"

Chapter seven

"Come in, gents," said Darren genially, ushering the two journalists into the lounge, where Sharren, wearing a long white gown with an ornate beaded collar, was draped along a sofa. Sharren had a thick black wig on her head and she'd painted her eyes with heavy eyeliner to make herself look like an Ancient Egyptian queen. She was determined to be in all the photos.

The two journalists walked over to her. One was short and stout and clutched a notebook in his hand; the other was tall and skinny and carried a camera over his shoulder.

"Cor!" said the tall, skinny one, peering closely at Sharren. "Is this it? Looks ancient!"

"Don't be stupid, Colin," hissed the

66

short, stout one. "This must be the lady of the house. You will excuse Colin, Mrs Brussell. He likes his little joke. Allow me to introduce my associate, Colin Carter, prize-winning photographer for *Mummies Monthly* . . ."

Sharren rose majestically from the sofa. Colin Carter, prize-winning photographer, jumped in alarm.

"It's alive!" he shouted. "Ouch!" he yelled, as his tubby colleague stood on his toes.

"Sorry, Colin, was that your foot?" The little journalist smiled an unpleasant smile and held out a podgy hand to Sharren. "I'm Clive Carnarvon – please call me Clive."

George mooched into the room, invisibly followed by Tootingkommon and the little band of ghosts. Tooting-kommon was sharper round the edges now that he was back in the house and nearer his coffin, but he was looking anxious about its fate.

"This is our boy," said Darren. He

chuckled. "He wants us to send the coffin back to Egypt!"

Clive Carnarvon gave George a shifty look. George frowned back as the journalist turned his expression into a smarmy smile and put his arm round George's shoulder.

"No point, lad," he said, in an oily voice. "They're two a penny out there."

"And there's loads of them," added Colin solemnly.

"Anyway," said Clive Carnarvon, "our magazine will be only too happy to buy an Egyptian coffin like yours and donate it to a museum. We're all heart at *Mummies Monthly*."

Colin was looking confused. "But we haven't got any money . . ."

"*Mummies*, Colin," interrupted Clive hastily. "We haven't got any *mummies* at the moment."

Suddenly the ghost pharaoh gave a strangled cry and pointed across the lounge.

"Mumsie!" he shouted. "I knew I'd find you!" He launched himself stiffly at Sharren.

"No!" called George. "That's *my* mum ... I think!"

Sharren howled with laughter. "This costume *must* be good if it's fooled Georgie!" she shrieked, as she adjusted her heavy beaded collar and twiddled her bangles. "Now, what about these photos? Shall we do the coffin first and then come down here for refreshments and photographs of me in my Elizabethan lounge, then me in my dining room, and of course, me in the master bedroom ... ?"

She led them away towards the tower staircase. The ghostly mummy turned to George.

"You're right," he said dejectedly. "Mumsie never sounded like that."

The two journalists stood, gobsmacked, in front of Tootingkommon's magnificent coffin.

"This will fetch a lot of money!" sighed Clive Carnarvon.

"And it's worth a packet," added Colin helpfully.

Clive whipped out a tape measure and measured the width of the coffin.

"Our readers like these little details," he told Darren.

George leaned against a wall and gloomily watched Clive Carnarvon sniffing round the room. The ghosts were downstairs in Darren's study. Both Edgar Jay and Tootingkommon had flatly refused to be hauled up the stairs again. Flo was in charge as they searched through the Internet for references to Egypt.

Clive Carnarvon put his tape across one of the window frames and shook his head. He caught George's eye. "Just checking how much light there is for the pictures," he explained quickly.

Sharren posed by the coffin as Colin stuck the camera in front of his face and clicked a button.

"Good camera that," called George rudely. "Takes pictures through the lens cap."

Colin stared at his camera, mouth open. "Ow!" he yelled, as his colleague kicked him on the leg.

"Sorry, Colin," said Clive Carnarvon, snapping off the lens cap. "Was that your shin?" He scowled at George and then remembered himself and smirked instead. "Well spotted, young man. I can see you don't miss much. Now tell me, Mr Brussell, what were your first thoughts on seeing this magnificent antiquity?"

With plenty of helpful interruptions from Sharren, Darren gave him the story. Clive Carnarvon scribbled in his otherwise empty notebook and Colin took a few pictures. Out of the corner of his eye, George saw a piece of ghostly paper flutter into the room. It stopped for a moment as if in fright, then charged over to George and hung quivering in front of his eyes.

Progress downstairs as I see it
by Bartholomew Otherington-Smythe

1. *Flo is teaching King Tootingkommon to play Militant Martians on the computing machine.*
2. *Maggot is arguing with her because he believes it is his turn.*
3. *His Majesty is becoming rather irritated because this is not helping him to find his home.*
4. *And he keeps hitting ten keys at a time.*
5. *Mary and Duck are re-enacting their famous victory at the Battle of Salty Bay.*
6. *Edgar Jay is redistributing the dust around*

the room.

7. *Slightly is asleep in the fax tray.*

8. *And I have brought you this list.*

9. *On my own.*

10. *Aren't I brave!*

George sighed. He couldn't trust the Little Terrors to do anything by themselves. He was heading for the door when his attention was caught by Colin. The photographer was tiptoeing carefully over the floorboards and stopping, with a foot in the air, each time he heard one creak.

"Colin!" snapped Clive.

"Sorry, Mr Carnarvon," said Colin. "Just getting ready for tonight's . . ."

". . . Line dancing," interrupted Clive. "Colin goes line dancing on Saturday nights." Colin looked puzzled. "*Don't you, Colin!*"

Colin nodded hastily. "If you say so, Mr Carnarvon."

"Now, Mr and Mrs Brussell," continued Clive smoothly, "if you would be so good as to step downstairs and prepare the lounge, we'll be with you in a second."

"Come on, Georgie," said his mother as she followed Darren out of the room. "I hope your room's tidy. They'll be wanting to take pictures of your four-poster. And have you been eating upstairs?" she hissed. "There's jam all over my banisters."

As George left the room, the door was shut behind him and he heard an agonized yell and a "Sorry, Colin, was that your knee?" All the way down the stairs his mum and dad were busy arguing about whether they wanted the moose head or the piano in the photos, so George sneaked off to Darren's study before they got him tidying his bedroom. Seven little spectres virtually disappeared with fright as he burst in and slammed the door.

"Come on, you lot," he shouted, stepping over Slightly's scuttling figure. "Dad's probably agreeing a price for the coffin at this very minute. This is no time for games."

"But it's my turn to kill the Martians!" wailed Maggot, trying to snatch the mouse from Flo.

"No it's not!" shouted Flo, hanging on grimly.

"It is!"

"It's not!"

"Is!"

"Isn't!"

"If you do not stop bickering," said Tootingkommon in a kingly fashion, "I will feed you both to the crocodiles. My coffin is in peril. I order you all to . . . to . . . *do* something!"

"That ain't much of a plan," sneered Mary. "More of a damp squib, if you ask me."

"Damp squid!" squawked Duck.

"Look!" squeaked Slightly suddenly. "There's a list. Under the door."

He snuffled round a ghostly scrap of paper that now lay on the carpet. Edgar Jay blew it over to Flo, who read it.

My situation on the other side of the door as I see it

by Bartholomew Otherington-Smythe

1. I am on the other side of the door.
2. Coincidentally, this is the second time in as many minutes that I have been on the wrong side of a door.
3. Firstly, I was shut in the tower room with Messrs Carter and Carnarvon.
4. Now I am here.
5. I would be grateful if you would let me in.
6. I have an urgent list to prepare.

"Why didn't you say so in the first place?" said George, flinging open the door. He could see the backs of the journalists as they joined his parents in the lounge.

A rapid list appeared on Darren's desk blotter.

Urgent List prepared by Bartholomew Otherington-Smythe

1. The journalists are crooks in disguise.
2. I heard their dastardly plan.

3. *They are coming back tonight to steal the coffin.*
4. *Oh dear!*

"Two masked men in their stripy vests," squawked Duck. "Yo ho ho and a bag of swag!"

"By the beak of Horus!" wailed Tooting-kommon. "Who knows what they will do with my coffin and me? Sell us at a bazaar like mere trinkets? Turn us into a cupboard? Use us as a doorstop?"

"Make a nice rowing boat," muttered Mary.

"Mary!" hissed Flo. "We're meant to be helping Tootingkommon."

Mary scowled. The nine-year-old scourge of the Spanish Main had never helped a king in her life and she wasn't going to start now.

"Don't worry, Toot," declared George. "I thought there was something fishy about Carter and Carnarvon. Whatever they're planning, they're not going to get away with it!"

Chapter Eight

The grandfather clock in the stone hall clonked the hour. It was three in the morning. Two shadowy figures stood outside the tower room door.

"It's shut tight," hissed the short, stout one, trying the door handle. "You'll have to pick it . . . Not your nose, Colin – the lock!"

Colin Carter could open almost anything, from the back door that was now letting in the fog, to the safest safe in the Little Frightley savings bank. This was the only reason Clive Carnarvon had taken on his dim accomplice. If Clive could stop Colin blurting out their plans beforehand, they usually got away with their robberies.

There was the sound of a nappy pin in the keyhole . . . and the door swung open.

Clive shone his torch around the dark room and lit up the golden coffin.

"Right, Colin," he whispered. "We don't have to worry about Mr and Mrs Brussell, they're on the other side of the house, and the servants sleep up in the attic flat. Mrs Brussell was most helpful with the layout of Little Frightley Manor. But don't forget the squeaking floorboards – we mustn't wake the boy. His bedroom's just below here and he's the sort who gets in the way."

He chuckled. "Lucky they fell for the *Mummies Monthly* rubbish. I thought I was very quick, thinking that up in the pub."

"Isn't there any *Mummies Monthly* then?" asked Colin, scratching his head.

"Course not, you idiot."

"Then who do I work for?"

Just then a floorboard creaked. It sounded very loud in the dark room.

"I told you to be careful!" hissed Clive.

"It wasn't me, Mr Carnarvon," whispered Colin, who hadn't moved a muscle. There was another creak. Clive swatted Colin round the head.

"Sorry, Colin," he smirked. "Was that your brain? No, it couldn't have been. You haven't got one! Now keep quiet and let's get this beauty out of here. We know it's too wide for the window so it's got to go down the stairs. You take the head, Colin . . . *Colin*?"

Colin Carter was staring dumbly over his tubby colleague's shoulder and pointing with a trembling finger at a jewelled dagger that was hanging in the air. As Clive turned to look, the dagger disappeared into the shadows. He shone his torch round the gloomy room.

"What's the matter with you, Colin?" he hissed. "There's nothing there – except for those old crates. Let's get on with it."

He strode over to the coffin. Behind him, three stuffed monkeys floated out of the darkness and waved at Colin. He yelped, and the monkeys vanished.

Clive Carnarvon shone his torch in his sidekick's face.

"You'll wake the Brussells if you carry on like that," he whispered fiercely. "And you know what happened to my last accomplice that mucked up a job, don't you, Colin?"

"Yes, Mr Carnarvon," gasped Colin. "But I saw ghost gorillas! I could even smell bananas . . ."

His jaw dropped open as the dis-embodied head of a demon, with ghastly staring eyes and wild hair blowing in a ghostly gust of air, popped briefly out of the gloom.

"It's horrible here!" yelled Colin in terror. "I want to go home."

"Any more of this and you'll never see home again," snarled Clive. "Get lifting!"

He grabbed the coffin, but Colin didn't move. He was now staring aghast at a piece of toilet paper that had suddenly appeared in his hand. He had trouble reading it as his hand was shaking, the ink was running and some of the words had more than one syllable. Clive snatched it from him and read it out.

Your situation as I see it
by A Mysterious Figure

1. *Beware the curse of the pharaoh's coffin.*
2. *He who attempts to purloin it will suffer the consequences.*
3. *Flee while you are still able!*

"I think a ghost wrote it," quavered Colin.

"I don't believe in ghosts!" snapped Clive. "The boy did it."

"I'm scared, Mr Carnarvon."

"I don't believe in being scared."

Suddenly, with a dreadful creaking, the lid of the coffin began to open and a yellow light seeped through the widening gap. Both thieves stared in dumb-struck terror as, wrapped from head to toe in bloodstained bandages and with its arms stretched menacingly towards them, out stepped an Egyptian mummy. Its ragged mouth slowly opened.

"I curse you," it croaked hideously. "By the nostrils of Nut, I will make you wish you had never disturbed the ghost of King Tootingkommon. You will meet your fate at the hands of an avenging fury who will smite you with a rod of iron." A poker appeared in the air. The mummy gave a bloodcurdling wail. So did the robbers. But as the deathly figure lurched towards them, it tripped over one of its loose bandages.

"Whoops," it said, as a bicycle lamp, covered in yellow tissue paper, clattered to the floor. The poker wobbled and vanished into the shadows.

"Ooooh!" wailed the mummy, hopefully. "Oooooooh?"

"Well, well, well," sneered Clive, touching a bloodstain on the bandages and licking his finger. "Tomato ketchup – and torn-up bed sheets. Who have we here?" He grabbed the figure and unwrapped its head. "Ah, it's young George – or should I say, little Lord Nosey-Parker. Just as I thought."

"No, you didn't," shouted George bravely as he twisted in the tubby thief's iron grasp. "You were petrified."

"Not half as petrified as you're going to be," growled Clive.

"And you'll be scared as well," added Colin. He wanted to ask George how he'd done the trick with the monkeys, but

84

thought it was safer not to.

Clive swiftly and expertly tied George up with his own bandages. Unlike Phatchops, Clive Carnarvon hadn't done any first-aid badges but he was experienced in restraining awkward people who got in his way. Phatchops would have been very impressed if he'd seen the result, and would have offered to show him the pyramid with the best drop.

"Help!" yelled George at the top of his voice.

"I'll give you curses and avenging furies!" snarled Clive, as he clapped a pudgy hand over George's mouth. "You'll wish you'd never tangled with Carnarvon and Carter!" Then he suddenly smiled. "Now, Colin," he said pleasantly, "what shall we do with our young friend?"

Colin looked blank.

"That's a good idea, Colin. We'll silence the little scallywag."

George tried in vain to bite Clive Carnarvon's hand.

"Shall I put a sock in his mouth?" asked his thick accomplice hopefully, bending down to undo his shoe. George wriggled in disgust.

"No, Colin," said Clive in a hushed tone. "I mean . . . *permanently*."

"Oh, sticky tape then."

"Shut up, you stupid fool!" snapped Clive. "Shove him in the coffin. We'll deal with him later . . . Come to think of it, we won't have to. There aren't any air holes!"

When George had first hidden in the

86

coffin, he had taken the precaution of wedging it slightly open with a bit of old doughnut which was now stuck on the bottom of Colin's shoe.

"It's all gone wrong," whispered Flo as the ghosts cowered behind the crate of treasures and watched a writhing and yelling George being bundled into the coffin.

"We haven't much time!" wheezed Edgar Jay. "Young Master George will run out of air."

"Attack the enemy!" shouted Mary, dropping the poker and drawing her cutlass.

"Set the crocodiles on them!" ordered King Tootingkommon, quivering in the shadows.

"Loose the cannons!" squawked Duck, desperately.

"Great idea, Duck!" yelled Maggot. "Let's launch the monkeys!" The ghosts started scrabbling about in the crate, looking for missiles.

The thieves grunted as they lifted the heavy coffin with its unwilling occupant whose yells were turning to gasps.

"Mind your heads!" cackled Duck as he swooped down, dropping bits of broken china on them.

Tootingkommon struggled stiffly to lift a portrait of someone's great-aunt that Sir Albert had acquired on one of his expeditions. Flo opened a box of cutlery, and Maggot heaved a monkey into the air.

"How's the boy doing that from inside the coffin?" asked Colin admiringly as a soup ladle hit him on the ear and a gust of air blew up his trouser leg.

"Shut up and keep heaving," panted Clive, dodging a silver cruet set. "Come on. Get that door open."

"Stop the murderous swabs!" shouted Mary, bounding to the door.

"I can't hear George any more!" yelled Flo. "I think we're too late!"

At that moment the door of the tower room was flung open, and there stood a monster with big staring eyes, yellow hair sprouting everywhere, and a deathly white painted face. It opened its mouth wide and let out an ear-piercing shriek. The two robbers dropped the coffin. The apparition lifted a rod of iron and went for Colin.

"Help!" shouted Colin. "It's the offending fury . . . I mean the avenging brewery . . . It's the curse of the mummy!"

The monster turned on Clive, who tried to fend off the blows with his torch. He

staggered back and yelped as something sharp stabbed him in the ankle.

"That'll stop you!" squeaked Slightly, jabbing at him with his hatpin.

Clive had just decided that as he wasn't going to get away with the robbery he might as well make a dash for it, when the portrait of somebody's great-aunt suddenly smashed down over his head. He struggled furiously but he was wedged tight in the heavy wooden frame.

"Touch my coffin, would you?" shrieked the avenging fury, as she lifted her rod again.

Darren appeared in the doorway, puffing breathlessly and shining a powerful flashlight. He gawped at the scene that met his eyes. The Egyptian coffin was lying on its side, and a mummified George was gasping for breath on the floor. The reporter from *Mummies Monthly* was encased in a picture frame, and his photographer was gibbering in a corner and shouting for the police to come and rescue him. Over them stood his wife in her dressing gown, with wild hair and facial night cream, and her arm raised ready to strike.

"Sharren darling!" gasped Darren. "Be careful, my love . . . That's my best golf club!"

Chapter Nine

"Had a busy time last night, did we?" said Mrs Duster, looking round the table and beaming. "Must have been tired – you even missed your breakfast. Look, boyo, there's a nice big plate of muffins for you."

"Thanks, Mrs D," said George, as she bustled out. He and the ghosts tucked in. "Hey, Toot, get your chops round these," he called across the breakfast room to where Tootingkommon was gazing sadly at a biscuit barrel with a picture of pyramids and camels on it.

"Ghosts don't eat," said the pharaoh mournfully.

"Ghosts don't *need* to eat," corrected Flo, stuffing another piece of muffin in her mouth where it immediately vanished, "but it's fun."

"Be there any fairy cakes?" demanded

Mary, flicking some crumbs on to the table. Edgar Jay blew them over to Duck and Slightly.

"Hearty rations!" squawked Duck, hopefully.

A dejected Tootingkommon fingered a muffin.

"You know, if all else fails," said George kindly, "you can always live here with us."

"We've got plenty of room in our caravan," added Maggot. "There's a spare bunk under your hammock, isn't there, Mary?"

"There's always room for a brave ghost," admitted Mary, grudgingly.

This was praise indeed from Mary Ghoulstone, scourge of the Spanish Main and expert raider of royal fleets. After last night, she realized King Tootingkommon was a brave soul who didn't seem to mind pirates and didn't stop to think of his own safety before capturing enemies, with picture frames. And anyway, she'd found out he didn't have any treasure on him.

"Georgie!" came a familiar shriek from

the doorway. The ghosts covered their ears as Sharren tottered into the room in her high-heeled fur mules, followed by Darren with his golf club.

"How's my little have-a-go hero?" shrilled Sharren proudly, giving George's cheek a squeeze.

George winced. He still had a bump on his head where the coffin had been dropped, and running out of air was not his idea of heroism.

"Leave the boy alone, Sharren," said Darren crossly, plonking himself down on a chair and sending a ghostly list flying. "I'm furious with the pair of you!" He picked up his golf club and began to inspect it for damage. "Tearing up the best bed sheets," he grumbled, "and using my new number five iron. Let the police deal with it next time."

"Rubbish!" screeched Sharren. "I'm just hoping *Mummies Monthly* get my photos done before those two villains go to prison."

"I've been telling you all morning, there's no such magazine," Darren said grumpily, as he struggled to straighten the kinks in his club. "That coffin's been more trouble than it's worth. I'm getting rid of it myself."

The ghosts looked at Darren in horror.

"But I want to go home!" wailed Tootingkommon, wobbling violently in his agitation.

"You could send the coffin back to Egypt," said George quickly. "I'll find out . . ."

"Don't interfere, son," said Darren firmly. "It's sorted. I'm donating it to the Little Frightley Museum. They sounded most interested on the phone and said they'd put a large plaque on it, mentioning my generosity. Mr Duster and I have just brought it down from the tower."

"My coffin!" howled Tootingkommon. "By the tears of Sobek, I must go with it or perish!"

"But, Dad!" gasped George. "You can't send it away! What about his family?"

95

"Mr Duster's family won't mind," said Darren puzzled. "That's what he's paid for."

"Then we're coming too," declared George, leaping to his feet.

"Speak for yourself," sniffed Sharren. "I wouldn't be seen dead in any dusty old museum." She settled down with a pile of magazines and a cup of coffee.

"Yes, speak for yourself, George," sniffed Flo. "We *might* be seen dead in a dusty old museum – and anyway, you know we go all wobbly away from home."

Little Frightley Museum was not dusty at all. It was a small, neat, grey-stone building in the middle of the village. Darren pulled up at the front. Tootingkommon had only just managed to get into his coffin with George's help before it had been heaved up on to the roof-rack. George had to make sure that once the coffin was on display, it was open, so that at least the ghost pharaoh could go for walks. He had a horrible, empty, achy feeling in his stomach, despite the muffins. He knew that Tootingkommon would be desperately lonely – he'd have to visit him as often as he could. He climbed slowly out of the car as Darren went off to find the curator.

"Avast there, George!"

There was Mary on the roof-rack, waving her cutlass at him.

"Cast anchor!" squawked Duck from her shoulder.

George couldn't believe his eyes.

"I thought you'd stayed at home!" he exclaimed. "Won't you go all wobbly?"

"Had to bid farewell to a worthy shipmate," growled Mary.

"We'll be all right if we're quick," said Flo.

"Short visit," squeaked Slightly from inside Maggot's shirt.

Flo lowered Edgar Jay, who had his nozzle over his eyes and was looking decidedly green. He hated going any faster than hoovering speed.

A piece of paper floated down in front of George.

King Tootingkommon's situation as I see it by Bartholomew Otherington-Smythe

1. *His Majesty is going to be very lonely here without his family.*
2. *We have decided to keep him company.*

"Oh, no!" said George, horrified at the thought of his ghostly friends leaving Little Frightley Manor.

3. But never fear, George, we shall not be leaving Little Frightley Manor.

4. With the help of you and your bicycle, we intend to take it in turns to visit His Majesty in his new home.

5. For ten minutes at a time.

6. Every day.

7. I will devise a rota system.

"That's a very kind idea," said George weakly, appalled at all the cycling he would have to do.

George and the ghosts followed as the coffin was carried carefully into one of the exhibition rooms, past a row of wooden statues and a display case of elaborate jewellery, and was propped up next to three other open coffins containing mummies. Darren took the curator aside to discuss the size of the promised plaque. When George was sure no one was looking, he heaved open the coffin lid. Tootingkommon lurched stiffly out.

"Here we are," said George, trying to

99

sound jolly. "Your new home. I'm sure you'll be happy here."

But the little pharaoh's eye slits were shut tight.

"I can't bear to look," he said miserably. "By the howl of Anubis, do not leave me here alone, for all eternity."

"We'll come and visit you," George assured him. "Every day!" He felt sick at the thought of Tootingkommon being left alone, for ever.

All of a sudden there was a window-rattling shriek from the other side of the room.

"My baby!" came a shrill, piercing voice. George and his ghostly friends put their fingers in their ears. "Tootsie darling! It's you! At last!"

The ghost of a vast Egyptian queen, flowing with bracelets and beads, emerged from behind a stone statue and held out her arms to the little pharaoh.

Tootingkommon opened his eyes. "Mumsie!" he yelled, staggering into her embrace.

"Klappumkommon! Ramesestreet!" sobbed his mother loudly. "Look who's come home!"

The ghost of a noble pharaoh, with a dazzling blue and gold head-dress, and an Egyptian princess in a white robe and jewelled headband, came gliding over and hugged their long-lost son and brother.

Tootingkommon turned to George and the ghosts, who were standing wide-eyed in amazement at the scene. "Thank you for bringing me home," he said simply.

"But . . . but . . . I thought you came from Egypt?" said George. "This is the local museum."

"Whatever it is, this is my home."

Tootingkommon was right. After 3,247 years stuck in his coffin in the family pyramid in the Valley of the Kings, he and his family had been discovered and brought to Britain. It was here that the coffins were opened for the first time and the ghostly royal family emerged. They had no idea they'd moved and were now in the Egyptian room of the Little Frightley Museum. They had no idea that so many years had gone by, as ghosts are very hazy about time passing. Tootingkommon's body had turned to dust shortly after Phatchops's embalming, and no one noticed it being swept up by the museum charlady.

Just five years later, in 1922, Sir Albert Ghoulstone made a night-time visit to the museum with his henchman, Vic, and

nicked the coffin of Tootingkommon, trapping the ghostly pharaoh who was inside at the time. In case anyone asked any awkward questions, Sir Albert was ready with his story – he'd just returned from Egypt and had been given the valuable artefact for rescuing King Fuad from the jaws of a crocodile. Tootingkommon was stuck in his coffin again, so, as his mother wasn't there to shriek him awake in the mornings, he had had another kip, groaning in his dreams now and then, until George and his friends released him.

"Shiver me feathers!" squawked Duck, fluttering up to perch on a jackal-headed statue, as a ghostly cat suddenly pounced and almost caught his blue tail. Slightly, who was just about to hibernate in the lap of the crocodile god, curled up into a frightened tube.

"Cleopetra!" yelled Tootingkommon. The cat twined herself lovingly round his legs, clawed her way up his bandages and nestled on his shoulder, where she kept a greedy eye on the parrot.

"This is so lovely!" boomed Kommonasmuk. "We're all together again!"

"I thought you said your mother was nothing like mine," whispered George, wincing.

"She isn't," hissed Tootingkommon. "Your mother is much quieter!"

George suddenly realized that his ghostly friends were fading.

"Come on," he said, "I'd better get you back."

"OK, son," called Darren, shaking the curator's hand. "Be with you in a minute."

"Not yet, Master George," wheezed Edgar Jay, wiping a tear away with his nozzle. "This is such a happy ending."

"I think we'd better," said Flo reluctantly. "My toes are feeling numb."

"And my nose has gone so weedy," wailed Maggot, "I can't even sniff."

"Blunt at the edges," whimpered the

hedgehog, unrolling and flexing his slightly flat prickles.

As they waved goodbye to Tooting-kommon and followed Darren out, a very faint list was pushed into the mummy's outstretched hand.

An Amended Visitors' Rota
by Bartholomew Otherington-Smythe

1. *Hurrah!*
2. *Your Majesty has been reunited with his family.*
3. *We will still visit, of course.*
4. *But we must preserve our spectral stuffing.*
5. *And George's cycling legs.*
6. *So we will not visit every day.*
7. *Sadly.*
8. *We will come every other day instead.*

Jan Burchett & Sara Vogler
LITTLE TERRORS 4:
Knight Frights

George and the Little Terrors are dead chuffed when they
discover armour-clad spook, Sir Arnold de Ghoulstone, walled up
in the cellar.

But George's welcome party for Sir Arnold's old soldiers goes
disastrously wrong. Not only are the ghost-guests monstrously
mangled – they also have murder on their minds!

Collect all the LITTLE TERRORS books!

JAN BURCHETT & SARA VOGLER

1. Hector the Spectre	0 330 36812 5	£2.99
2. Eerie McLeery	0 330 36813 3	£2.99
3. Bones and Groans	0 330 36815 X	£2.99
4. Knight Frights	0 330 36814 1	£2.99

MORE LITTLE TERRORS BOOKS FOLLOW SOON!
